Owls

Emily Bone

Designed by Sam Chandler

Illustrated by Jenny Cooper and Richard Watson

Owl expert: Rob Hume
Reading consultant: Alison Kelly, Principal Lecturer,
University of Roehampton

Contents

Night birds

Owls are birds with big eyes and pointed beaks. Most owls are nocturnal. This means they're awake during the evening and at night.

This is a great grey owl hunting for food.

Owls live in almost every country in the world.

Living at night

Owls have different ways to help them find their way when there's not much light.

Ear

Their big eyes help them to see in the dark much better than most animals.

Their sensitive ears can tell exactly where things are moving around them.

Most owls fly to the same places each night, so they never get lost.

Owls can turn their heads around, so they can see in all directions.

This screech owl is looking behind itself.

The tufts on its head are feathers, not ears. No one really knows why owls have them.

Hot and cold

Owls live in many different types of places.

This is an eagle owl. It lives in a very cold place.

Its thick feathers trap heat next to its skin.

It has feathers all over its legs and feet, too.

Owls also live in countries where it is very warm. They find ways to keep cool.

Some owls live in thick forests where trees shade them from the hot sun.

In hot places where there are no trees, owls rest in burrows or caves.

Owls that live near rivers or lakes splash around in the water to cool down.

Owls cool down quickly by panting and holding out their wings.

Super hunters

Many owls eat small animals such as mice, voles and birds. Owls catch their prey quickly and quietly.

An owl sits very still in a tree, listening and watching for animals on the ground.

As soon as it spots a bird, the owl flies down towards it, feet first.

The bird can't hear the owl coming because it's so quiet.

This barred owl is about to grab a mouse using powerful claws, known as talons.

After it has caught the mouse, the owl will swallow it whole.

Hunting

Owls hunt in different ways.

Barn owls fly low over fields looking for small animals to eat.

When the owl finds an animal, it hovers above it, like this. Then it swoops down to grab it.

As a fish owl flies over a lake or a river, it pulls a fish out of the water.

It takes the fish back to a rock, rips it into pieces, then swallows it.

A burrowing owl hunts by chasing insects, lizards and small animals.

It uses its long legs to run after a lizard, catches it, then eats it.

An elf owl snatches moths out of the air and eats them while it's flying.

Hidden owls

Owls have patterns on their feathers that help them to hide while they're hunting or sleeping.

This is a snowy owl. It lives where the land is often covered with snow. It hunts during the day.

Its white feathers make it difficult to spot. The animals that it hunts can't see it coming.

Most owls sleep during the day. They hide so they're not attacked by other animals.

A boreal owl's feathers look like bark so it stays hidden in trees.

The tufts of feathers on a scops owl's head make it look like a broken branch.

Short eared owls sleep in long grass.

Owl talk

Owls make sounds, known as calls.
Different types of owls have different calls.

This is a great grey owl. It makes a loud
crying call to scare away other animals.

Owls also call to find a mate.

'Hoo, hoo-oo'

'Ke-wick!'

A male tawny owl makes a hooting call to let other owls know where he is.

A female owl hears the call. She replies to the male owl by calling 'ke-wick'.

'Hoo-ooo!'

The male answers by hooting loudly. This tells other male owls to go away.

The two owls keep calling to each other. Then the male goes to join the female.

High homes

Owls don't build nests.
Most find safe places high
off the ground to lay eggs
and look after their young.

Screech owls use
holes or cracks at
the tops of trees
where they can
keep a look out.

Some owls scare
other animals out
of their nests so
they can use them.

BOO!

Eagle owls find flat
ledges on the sides
of mountains to lay
their eggs.

Great horned owls
use old nests that
have been made
by other birds.

Elf owls live in the
desert. They lay
their eggs in holes
in desert plants.

Ground nesters

Some owls lay their eggs on or under the ground.

This burrowing owl has laid its eggs in a burrow that was dug by another animal.

The eggs are under the ground, away from animals that might eat them.

Snowy owls lay eggs on hard ground.

The mother owl uses her sharp talons to dig a hollow in the ground.

She collects feathers and grass to line the hollow, then lays her eggs on top.

The mother sits on the eggs. The father owl scares away attackers.

Owl babies

After a mother owl has laid her eggs, she sits on them to keep them warm.

She presses a warm, bare patch of skin, called a brood patch, onto the eggs.

The father owl hunts for food and brings it back to the mother.

The babies grow inside the eggs. After around 30 days, they hatch out.

The mother will then tear the food into pieces for the babies to swallow.

Baby owls are called owlets. They only have a few fluffy feathers.

These eagle owlets are around three weeks old. They are staying close to their mother to keep warm.

Growing up

As owlets grow, they start to explore the area around their homes.

These Ural owlets are resting on a branch near to where they hatched.

If you see an owlet on the ground, it's probably learning how to fly.

Burrowing owlets leave their burrows when they're around four weeks old.

The young owlets stay near their burrow. They're fed by their parents.

As the owlets get bigger, their parents teach them how to fly and hunt.

After two months, the owlets are fully grown. They can fly and feed themselves.

Big and small

Owls can be lots of different sizes.

Eagle owls are the biggest owls in the world. Their prey is big, too.

Eurasian eagle owls hunt many things, such as rabbits, fish and other birds.

Some eagle owls live in Africa. They eat small deer, monkeys and snakes.

Indian spot-bellied eagle owls grab sleeping birds from trees at night.

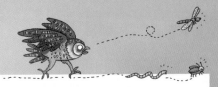

Small owls hunt very small things, such as insects and worms.

The pygmy owl is the smallest owl.

This is its actual size.

Owl enemies

Many owls are hunted by other animals and birds.

Some owls scare away attackers by making themselves look bigger. This great horned owlet has spread its wings.

Young owls hiss and snap their beaks to frighten away attackers.

Some owls fly into bigger birds and attack them with their feet.

Elf owls pretend to be dead so bigger animals leave them alone.

Where are they?

Owls can be difficult to spot, but there are ways that you can find them.

You might see some owls, like this short eared owl, hunting just before the sun sets.

At night, you are more likely to hear an owl calling than see it.

Hoo-ooo!

Hoo-ooo!

You can tell that an owl lives nearby if you find pellets on the ground.

Owls swallow every part of the animals, birds or insects they catch.

Then, they bring up the bones, fur or feathers as lumps, known as pellets.

If you look closely, you might see parts of the things that were eaten.

Glossary

Here are some of the words in this book you might not know. This page tells you what they mean.

 nocturnal - to be awake at night. Most owls are nocturnal.

 burrow - an underground tunnel where owls rest, hide or lay eggs.

 prey - the different things that are hunted by owls.

 talons - an owl's sharp claws.

 calls - sounds owls make to tell other owls and animals different things.

 owlet - a young owl, before it has grown adult feathers.

 pellets - lumps of bone, fur or feathers coughed up by owls.

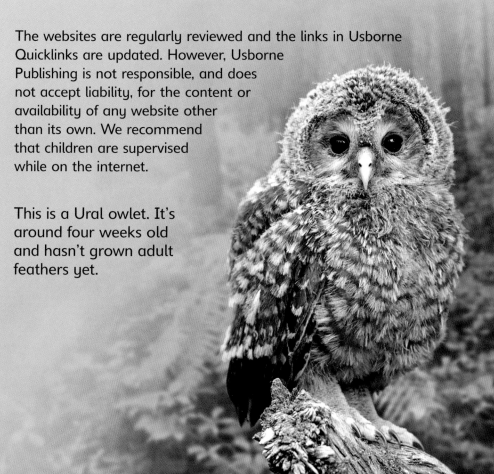

Websites to visit

You can visit interesting websites to find out more about owls.

To visit these websites, go to the Usborne Quicklinks Website at **www.usborne-quicklinks.com** Read the internet safety guidelines, and then type the keywords "**beginners owls**".

The websites are regularly reviewed and the links in Usborne Quicklinks are updated. However, Usborne Publishing is not responsible, and does not accept liability, for the content or availability of any website other than its own. We recommend that children are supervised while on the internet.

This is a Ural owlet. It's around four weeks old and hasn't grown adult feathers yet.

Index

Acknowledgements

Photographic manipulation by John Russell

Photo credits
The publishers are grateful to the following for permission to reproduce material:
cover © **Edwin Giesbers/naturepl.com**; p1© **Kim Taylor/naturepl.com**; p2-3 © **Harri Taavetti/FLPA**;
p4 © **Michael Nichols/Getty Images**; p5 © **Wayne Lynch/All Canada Photos/SuperStock**;
p6 © **imagebroker.net/SuperStock**; p9 © **Bruce J. Lichtenberger/Alaska Stock/SuperStock**;
p10 © **NHPA/Photoshot**; p12-13 © **James Urbach/SuperStock**; p14 © **Tier und Naturfotografie/
SuperStock**; p16 © **NHPA/Photoshot**; p18 © **Tier und Naturfotografie/SuperStock**; p21 © **Minden
Pictures/SuperStock**; p22 © **Clover/SuperStock**; p25 © **Rolf Nussbaumer/Imagebroker/FLPA**;
p26-27 © **Michael Quinton/Minden Pictures/FLPA**; p28 © **Andy Rouse/2020VISION/naturepl.com**;
p31 © **imagebroker.net/SuperStock**.

Every effort has been made to trace and acknowledge ownership of copyright. If any rights have
been omitted, the publishers offer to rectify this in any subsequent editions following notification.